CONTENTS

BABY, I LOVE YOUR WAY

Words and Music by
PETER FRAMPTON

But don't hes - i - tate, __ 'cause your

love _____ won't __ wait. _____

BEST OF MY LOVE

Words and Music by JOHN DAVID SOUTHER,
DON HENLEY and GLENN FREY

Moderately slow

mp legato

with pedal throughout

Ev-er-y night __ I'm ly-in' in bed, __ hold-in' you close __ in my
Beau-ti-ful faces and loud emp-ty places, look at the way that we

dreams; __ think-in' a-bout __ all the things that we __ said __ and
live; __ wast-in' our time __ on cheap talk and wine

BAND ON THE RUN

Words and Music by
McCARTNEY

16

Brighter beat

1. Well, the

rain ex - plod - ed with a might - y crash__ As we fell in - to__ the sun,__
un - der - tak - er drew a heav - y sigh__ See - ing no one else__ had come,__
night was fall - ing as the des - ert world__ Be - gan to set - tle down.__

And the first one said to the sec - ond one there__ I hope you're hav - ing fun.__
And a bell was ring - ing in the vil - lage square__ For the rab - bits on the run.__
In the town they're search - ing for us ev - 'ry where__ But we nev - er will be found.__

CAN'T YOU SEE

Words and Music by
TOY CALDWELL

CHICAGO

Words and Music by
GRAHAM NASH

23

* Male vocal written at actual pitch.

CRAZY LITTLE THING CALLED LOVE

Words and Music by
FREDDIE MERCURY

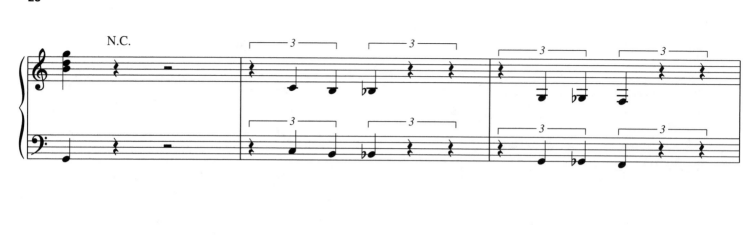

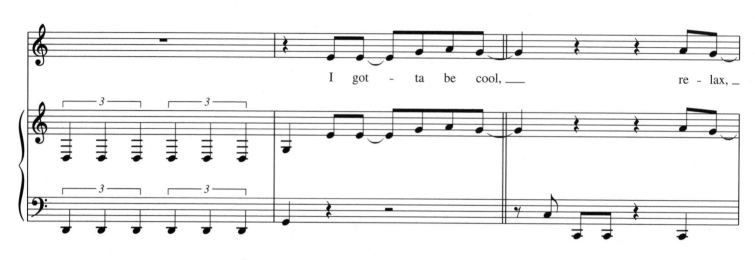

I got - ta be cool, ___ re - lax, ___

___ a - get hip, ___ a - get on my tracks. Take a

back seat, ___ hitch - hike ___ to take a lit - tle long _ ride ___ on my

CRAZY ON YOU

Words and Music by ANN WILSON,
NANCY WILSON and ROGER FISHER

Moderately fast Rock

We may still have time, __ we may still get by. __ Ev-'ry
love is the eve - ning breeze touch-ing your skin. __ The

time I think a - bout __ it, I __ want to cry. __ With bombs and the dev - il, and
gen - tle sweet sing - ing of leaves __ in the wind. __ The whis - per that calls __ af - ter

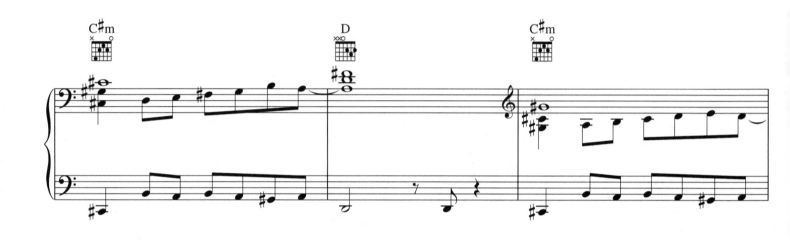

DARK HOLLOW

Words and Music by
BILL BROWNING

I'd rath-er be in

some dark hol-low where the sun don't

ev - er shine ___ than to be ___ { home a - lone, ___ in some ___

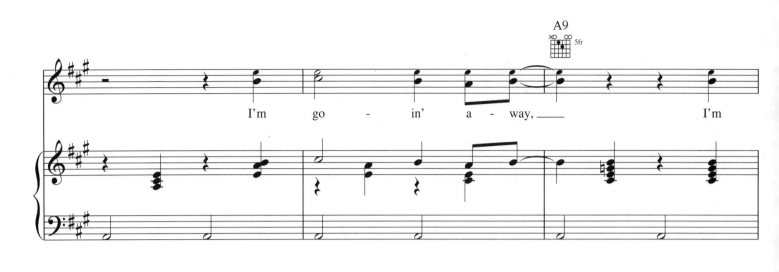

I'm go - in' a - way, _____ I'm

leav - in' to - day. _____ I'm go - in' but I ain't com - in' back.

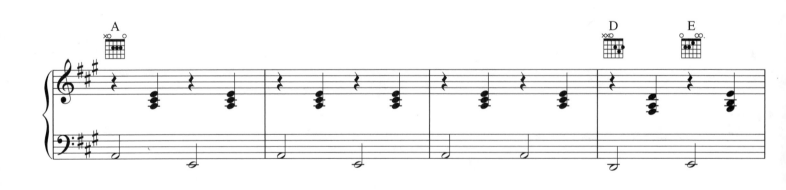

THE FLAME

Words and Music by BOB MITCHELL
and NICK GRAHAM

I will be ___ the flame. ___

FREE FALLIN'

Words and Music by TOM PETTY
and JEFF LYNNE

51

52

GIVE A LITTLE BIT

Words and Music by RICK DAVIES
and ROGER HODGSON

HELP ME MAKE IT THROUGH THE NIGHT

Words and Music by
KRIS KRISTOFFERSON

A GROOVY KIND OF LOVE

Words and Music by TONI WINE
and CAROLE BAYER SAGER

Slowly

When I'm feel-in'

blue, all I have to do is take a look at you, then I'm not so ____
want to, you can turn me on to an - y - thing you want to, an - y - time at ____

____ blue. When you're close to me, I can feel your heart beat, I can hear you
____ all. When I kiss your lips, ooh, I start to shiv - er, can't con - trol the

HEAVEN

Words and Music by BRYAN ADAMS
and JIM VALLANCE

68

HER TOWN TOO

Words and Music by JOHN DAVID SOUTHER,
JAMES TAYLOR and ROBERT WACHTEL

I'LL HAVE TO SAY I LOVE YOU
IN A SONG

Words and Music by
JIM CROC[...]

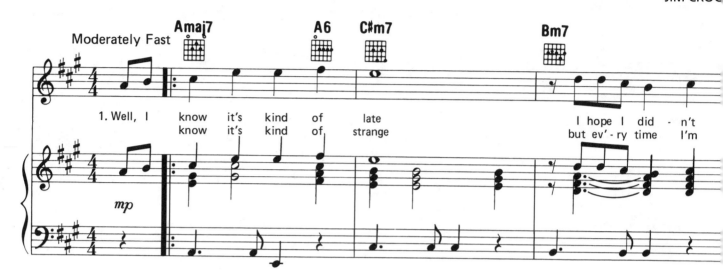

Moderately Fast

1. Well, I know it's kind of late
know it's kind of strange

I hope I did - n't
but ev'-ry time I'm

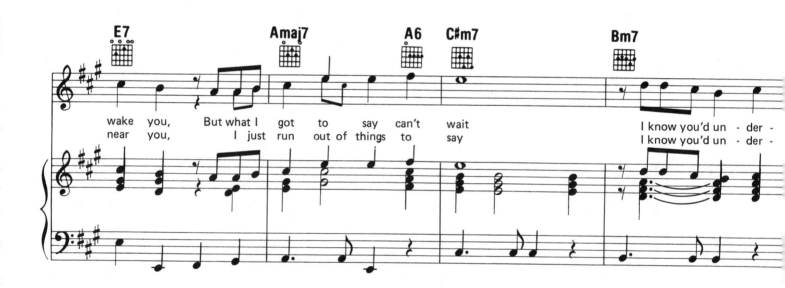

wake you,
near you,

But what I got to say can't wait
I just run out of things to say

I know you'd un - der -
I know you'd un - der -

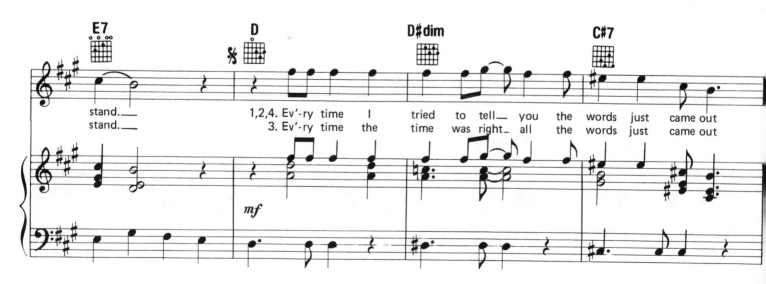

stand.___
stand.___

1,2,4. Ev'-ry time I tried to tell___ you the words just came out
3. Ev'-ry time the time was right___ all the words just came out

IF YOU LEAVE ME NOW

Words and Music by
PETER CETERA

-row comes, ___ then we'll both ___ re - gret ___ the things we said ___ to - day. ___

86

IT'S A HEARTACHE

Words and Music by RONNIE SCOTT
and STEVE WOLFE

JESSICA

Written by DICKEY BETTS

Copyright Renewed
All Rights Administered by Unichappell Music Inc.
International Copyright Secured   All Rights Reserved

D.S. al Coda
(take 2nd ending)

JUST A SONG BEFORE I GO

Words and Music by
GRAHAM NASH

NIGHTS IN WHITE SATIN

Words and Music by
JUSTIN HAYWARD

LEADER OF THE BAND

Words and Music by
DAN FOGELBERG

nough. The lead-er of the band _ is tired _ and _ his

leg - a - cy ___ to the lead - er of _____ the

band. __

MY SWEET LORD

Words and Music by
GEORGE HARRISON

OUR HOUSE

Words and Music by
GRAHAM NASH

PINK HOUSES

Words and Music by
JOHN MELLENCAMP

Moderate Rock

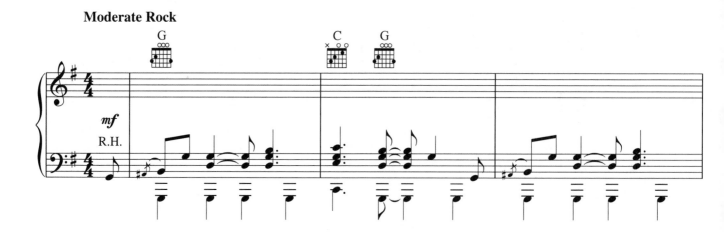

There's a black man with a black cat
young man in a T - shirt
peo - ple and more peo - ple.

liv - in' in a black neigh - bor - hood. _____ He's got an
lis - t'nin' to a rock - in' roll - in' sta - tion. ____ He's got
What do they know? _____

in - ter - state ___ run - nin' through ___ his front yard. ___ You know, he
greas - y hair ___ and a greas - y smile ___ that says, "Lord,
Go to work ___ in some high - rise and va - ca - tion down at

thinks he's got it so good. ___ And there's a
this must be my des - ti - na - tion." 'Cause they
the Gulf of Mex - i - co. ___ And there's

wom - an in the kitch - en clean - in' up the eve - nin' slop. ___
told me when I was young - er, "Boy, you gon - na be Pres - i -
win - ners and there's los - ers, but they ain't no big deal. ___

POETRY MAN

Words and Music by
PHOEBE SNOW

ROCKY MOUNTAIN HIGH

Words and Music by JOHN DENVER
and MIKE TAYLOR

Rock - y Moun - tain high,

Rock - y Moun - tain high.

He climbed

Now his

RUNNING ON FAITH

Words and Music by
JERRY WILLIAM

Late-ly, I've been run-nin' on _____ faith. ___
Late-ly, I've been talk - in' in ___ my sleep.

SAY YOU LOVE ME

Words and Music by
CHRISTINE McVIE

Brightly

Have mer - cy, ba - by, on ____
pit - y, ba - by, just ____
Ba - by, ba - by, hope

____ a poor girl like me. ____
____ when I thought it was o - ver.
you're gon - na stay a - way. ____

You know I'm fall - ing, fall - ing, fall -
Now you got me run - ning, run -
'Cause I'm get - ting weak - er, weak -

SHOW ME THE WAY

Words and Music by
PETER FRAMPTON

Moderately

I won - der how you're feel - ing. _____ There's

I can see no rea - son. _____ You're

SMALL TOWN

Words and Music by
JOHN MELLENCAMP

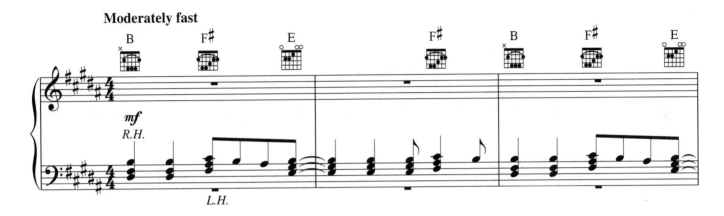

Well, I was born in a small town,
and I live in a small town;

Ed-u-cat-ed in a small town,
taught the fear of Je-sus in a small town;

prob-'ly die in a small
used to day-dream in that

SWEET TALKIN' WOMAN

Words and Music by
JEFF LYNNE

170

TEACH YOUR CHILDREN

Words and Music by
GRAHAM NASH

You who are on the road ___

172

174

TAKE ME HOME, COUNTRY ROADS

Words and Music by JOHN DENVER
BILL DANOFF and TAFFY NIVERT

179

THING CALLED LOVE
(Are You Ready for This Thing Called Love)

Words and Music by
JOHN HIATT

TIME FOR ME TO FLY

Words and Music by
KEVIN CRONIN

I've been a-round ___ for you, been up and down ___ for ___ you; but
You said we'd work ___ it out. You said that you had ___ no ___ doubt that

I just can't get an-y re-lief. ___
deep down we were real-ly in love. ___

I've
But

I make you laugh, _____ and _ you make me cry. _____

I be - lieve it's time _____ for me _____ to fly. _____

Time for me _____ to fly. _____ I've got to set _____ my - self free.

TIME IN A BOTTLE

Words and Music by
JIM CROCE

TWO OUT OF THREE AIN'T BAD

Words and Music by
JIM STEINMAN

YOU'RE IN MY HEART

Words and Music by
ROD STEWART

YOU'RE ONLY LONELY

Words and Music by
JOHN DAVID SOUTHER

Additional Lyrics

... it's no crime, we got lots of time.
Aw, there's nothing wrong with you. Darlin', I get lonely too.
So if you need me, all you gotta do is call me.
You're only lonely.

THE POP/ROCK ERA

Hal Leonard is proud to present these fantastic folios that gather the best popular songs from the '50s to today! All books arranged for piano, voice, and guitar.

THE POP/ROCK ERA: THE '50s

54 highlights from the first official decade of the pop/rock revolution, including: All Shook Up • At the Hop • Don't Be Cruel (To a Heart That's True) • Donna • Get a Job • Great Balls of Fire • Hound Dog • It's So Easy • Kansas City • (You've Got) Personality • That'll Be the Day • Why Do Fools Fall in Love • and more.
00310788..$14.95

THE POP/ROCK ERA: THE '60s

52 songs that helped shape the pop/rock era, including: Baby Love • Can't Take My Eyes off of You • Crying • Fun, Fun, Fun • Hey Jude • I Heard It Through the Grapevine • I Think We're Alone Now • Louie, Louie • Mony, Mony • Respect • Stand by Me • Stop! In the Name of Love • Wooly Bully • and more.
00310789..$14.95

THE POP/ROCK ERA: THE '70s

44 of the top songs from the '70s, including: ABC • Baby, I Love Your Way • Bohemian Rhapsody • Don't Cry Out Loud • Fire and Rain • I Love the Night Life • Imagine • Joy to the World • Just My Imagination (Running Away with Me) • The Logical Song • Oye Como Va • Piano Man • Three Times a Lady • We've Only Just Begun • You Are So Beautiful • and more.
00310790..$14.95

THE POP/ROCK ERA: THE '80s

38 top pop hits from the '80s, including: Back in the High Life Again • Centerfold • Every Breath You Take • Eye in the Sky • Higher Love •Summer of '69 • Sweet Dreams (Are Made of This) • Thriller • Time After Time • and more.
0031079..$14.95

THE POP/ROCK ERA: THE '90s

35 hits that shaped pop music in the 1990s, including: All I Wanna Do • Angel • Come to My Window • (Everything I Do) I Do It for You • Fields of Gold • From a Distance • Hard to Handle • Hero • I Will Remember You • Mambo No. 5 (A Little Bit Of...) • My Heart Will Go On (Love Theme from 'Titanic') • Ray of Light • Tears in Heaven • When She Cries • and more.
00310792..$14.95

Prices, contents and availability subject to change without notice.

www.halleonard.com

The Greatest Songs Ever Written

THE BEST EVER COLLECTION
ARRANGED FOR PIANO, VOICE AND GUITAR

150 of the Most Beautiful Songs Ever
150 ballads: Edelweiss • For All We Know • How Deep Is Your Love • I'll Be Seeing You • Summertime • Unchained Melody • Young at Heart • many more.
00360735..$19.95

The Best Big Band Songs Ever
Over 60 big band hits: Boogie Woogie Bugle Boy • Don't Get Around Much Anymore • In the Mood • Moonglow • Sentimental Journey • Who's Sorry Now • more.
00359129..$16.95

The Best Broadway Songs Ever
Over 70 songs in all! Includes: All I Ask of You • Bess, You Is My Woman • Climb Ev'ry Mountain • Comedy Tonight • If I Were a Rich Man • Ol' Man River • more!
00309155..$20.95

The Best Christmas Songs Ever
More than 60 holiday favorites: Frosty the Snow Man • A Holly Jolly Christmas • I'll Be Home for Christmas • Rudolph, The Red-Nosed Reindeer • Silver Bells • more.
00359130..$19.95

The Best Classic Rock Songs Ever
Over 60 hits: American Woman • Bang a Gong • Cold As Ice • Heartache Tonight • Rock and Roll All Nite • Smoke on the Water • Wonderful Tonight • and more.
00310800..$17.95

The Best Classical Music Ever
Over 80 of classical favorites: Ave Maria • Canon in D • Eine Kleine Nachtmusik • Für Elise • Lacrymosa • Ode to Joy • William Tell Overture • and many more.
00310674..$19.95

The Best Contemporary Christian Songs Ever
Over 70 favorites, including: Awesome God • El Shaddai • Friends • Jesus Freak • People Need the Lord • Place in This World • Serve the Lord • Thy Word • more.
00310558..$19.95

The Best Country Songs Ever
78 classic country hits, featuring: Always on My Mind • Crazy • Daddy Sang Bass • Forever and Ever, Amen • God Bless the U.S.A. • I Fall to Pieces • Stand By Your Man • Through the Years • and more.
00359135..$17.95

The Best Early Rock N Roll Songs Ever
Over 70 songs, including: Book of Love • Crying • Do Wah Diddy Diddy • Louie, Louie • Peggy Sue • Shout • Splish Splash • Stand By Me • Tequila • and more.
00310816..$17.95

The Best Easy Listening Songs Ever
75 mellow favorites: (They Long to Be) Close to You • Every Breath You Take • How Am I Supposed to Live Without You • Unchained Melody • more.
00359193..$18.95

The Best Gospel Songs Ever
80 gospel songs: Amazing Grace • Daddy Sang Bass • How Great Thou Art • I'll Fly Away • Just a Closer Walk with Thee • Just a Little Talk with Jesus • The Old Rugged Cross • Will the Circle Be Unbroken • more.
00310503..$19.95

The Best Hymns Ever
118 of the most loved hymns of all time: Abide with Me • Every Time I Feel the Spirit • He Leadeth Me • I Love to Tell the Story • The Old Rugged Cross • Were You There? • When I Survey the Wondrous Cross • and more.
00310774..$17.95

The Best Jazz Standards Ever
77 jazz hits: April in Paris • Don't Get Around Much Anymore • Love Is Here to Stay • Misty • Satin Doll • Unforgettable • When I Fall in Love • and more.
00311641..$18.95

The Best Latin Songs Ever
67 songs, including: Besame Mucho (Kiss Me Much) • Blame It on the Bossa Nova • The Girl from Ipanema • Malaguena • One Note Samba • Slightly Out of Tune (Desafinado) • Summer Samba (So Nice) • and more.
00310355..$19.95

The Best Love Songs Ever
65 favorite love songs, including: Endless Love • Here and Now • Love Takes Time • Misty • My Funny Valentine • So in Love • You Needed Me • Your Song.
00359198..$17.95

The Best Movie Songs Ever
74 songs from the movies: Almost Paradise • Chariots of Fire • My Heart Will Go On • Take My Breath Away • Unchained Melody • You'll Be in My Heart • more.
00310063..$19.95

The Best R&B Songs Ever
66 songs, including: Baby Love • Endless Love • Here and Now • I Will Survive • Saving All My Love for You • Stand By Me • What's Going On • and more.
00310184..$19.95

The Best Rock Songs Ever
Over 60 songs: All Shook Up • Blue Suede Shoes • Born to Be Wild • Every Breath You Take • Free Bird • Hey Jude • We Got the Beat • Wild Thing • more!
00490424..$18.95

The Best Songs Ever
Over 70 must-own classics, including: All I Ask of You • Crazy • Edelweiss • Love Me Tender • Memory • My Funny Valentine • Tears in Heaven • Unforgettable • The Way We Were • A Whole New World • and more.
00359224..$22.95

More of the Best Songs Ever
79 more favorites: April in Paris • Candle in the Wind • Endless Love • Misty • My Blue Heaven • My Heart Will Go On • Stella by Starlight • Witchcraft • more.
00310437..$19.95

The Best Standards Ever, Vol. 1 (A-L)
72 beautiful ballads, including: All the Things You Are • Bewitched • Getting to Know You • God Bless' the Child • Hello, Young Lovers • It's Only a Paper Moon • I've Got You Under My Skin • The Lady Is a Tramp.
00359231..$15.95

The Best Standards Ever, Vol. 2 (M-Z)
72 songs, including: Makin' Whoopee • Misty • Moonlight in Vermont • My Funny Valentine • People Will Say We're in Love • Smoke Gets in Your Eyes • Strangers in the Night • Tuxedo Junction • Yesterday.
00359232..$15.95

More of the Best Standards Ever, Vol. 1 (A-L)
76 all-time favorites, including: Ain't Misbehavin' • Always • Autumn in New York • Body and Soul • Desafinado • Fever • Fly Me to the Moon • For All We Know • Georgia on My Mind • Lazy River • and more.
00310813..$17.95

More of the Best Standards Ever, Vol. 2 (M-Z)
75 more stunning standards: Makin' Whoopee! • Mona Lisa • Mood Indigo • Moon River • My Favorite Things • Norwegian Wood • Route 66 • Sentimental Journey • Stella by Starlight • What a Diff'rence a Day Made • What'll I Do? • You Are the Sunshine of My Life • more.
00310814..$17.95

FOR MORE INFORMATION, SEE YOUR LOCAL MUSIC DEALER, OR WRITE TO:

HAL•LEONARD CORPORATION
7777 W. BLUEMOUND RD. P.O. BOX 13819 MILWAUKEE, WI 53213

Visit us on-line for complete songlists.
www.halleonard.com

Prices, contents and availability subject to change without notice. Not all products available outside the U.S.A.

0402

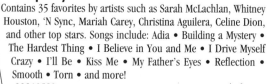